Making your marriage work: The ultimate guide for married couples.

Jonathan Pollock

Table of contents

Chapter 1

The reality about marriages

The earliest officially documented marriage occurred in Mesopotamia around 2350 B.C. Since that first couple uttered whatever form of "I do" they said, millions have sworn vows to permanently promise their lives to one another. After the vows are made and life settles in, truths emerge. About what it takes to sustain a good relationship. About the inevitable battles that will ensue. About why never having to say you're sorry is crap. About what it genuinely means to be a partner on good days, difficult days, and those days when the sound of your spouse's chewing makes you want to muzzle them.

Marriage is life, woven together. It contains, as it has been stated, multitudes. As such, we wanted to give some basic facts about marriage to raise the curtain, illuminate the road, and let you know that there are certain certainties everyone should bear in mind. Some of these realities are amusing; others are serious. All, we believe, shed some light on the inner workings of sharing your life with someone. Because although each marriage is the same, a lot of marriages — and essential values — are similar.

Everyone thinks of leaving. That's simply a part of remaining.
Forgiveness is for those you don't share a bed with. Forgetfulness is for individuals you do.
Not everything has to be equal. In truth, nothing ever truly is.
It's crucial to know what portions of your spouse need to be scratched from time to time.
Arguing before the coffee is a waste of time.
Talking about your lover behind their back is a wonderful thing. To be married is to require guidance.
But there's some information that your spouse will deem secret.

Don't assume that you have access to your partner's work life.

Sometimes sex is tiresome and boring and you're weary and not in the mood and that's a truth of life.

Having a child binds you, yes. You're doing it together and learning together. It will also lead to fierce power struggles and some of the most bare-knuckled brawls you never dreamed you'd experience. About stuff like the best technique to burp the infant, or what sort of cheese you should use in that seven-layer dip dish.

You will surely identify your marital troubles in family sitcoms which suggests that your marriage is not as exceptional as you probably thought it was.

There will come a day when the most frequent messages from your spouse will be "Can you pick up X from the grocery store?"

Anniversaries cease becoming special after year 10.

If you're not talking about sex — what makes your eyes roll back, what makes them simply roll — chances are it's not that fantastic.

At some point, you have to stop being "lovers" and start being colleagues who fuck sometimes.

Every married couple should speak about money a lot more frequently than they are.

A successful marriage can survive you being honest about your kink.

You will go to bed furious occasionally.

You will wake up irritated occasionally.

Remembering the tiny things will solve so many troubles. And marriage will make you understand that they're not genuinely tiny things. They're very, very huge things.

Sex will be frequent and occasionally mind-blowing. Then, for a while, it will be perfectly fine and not as frequent. Then it will be mind-blowing again.

You will hear your spouse relate the same tale 4587 times during the length of your marriage.

Your partner will panic about things that you believe are completely unreasonable.

Looking at such irrationalities as reasonable and treating them as such is crucial. You don't have to agree with them, but you do need to be empathetic. Emotional invalidation is a murderer.

There may be occasions when your spouse will disclose something from a former event that will startle you and remind you that you don't know them as well as you thought.

You will go out with other couples and think they are quirky or, honestly, the fucking worst. You will go out with couples that think the same of you.

Seemingly minor things — how someone puts the eggs in the fridge, the number of paper towels they use, whether they leave the cabinet doors open if they accidentally hog the blankets at night — will be the doorway to hour-long disagreements.

When your partner tells you they "accidentally" hogged the covers understand just what they're doing.

Talking trash about other couples will be considered a terrific date night.

You will, at some moment or another, feel that your spouse and the kids share a connection you could never have.

Without separate interests, stuff will go wrong.

Without regular things to do together, stuff will likewise go south.

There's some truth to this Ogden Nash adage, "Marriage is the tie between a person who never recalls anniversaries and another who never forgets them." Understanding how you complement one another is vital.

Marriages usually end badly. The best-case scenario is that someone dies in the end.

Divorce doesn't indicate that marriage was a failure. The journey has worth beyond the goal.

There's also validity to this one from Ben Franklin: "Keep your eyes wide open before marriage, half shut afterward." In other words, you have to take some things with a grain of salt.

Love doesn't just subsist on its own. It is maintained by activities.

Marriage will teach you, more than anything in life when to quiet up.

Comparison, it has been said, is the thief of joy. But you will compare yourself to others. It's nice to have perspective. It's also harmful to be covetous.

Having a sense of humor about things will take you far; understanding when not to make a joke will take you farther.

There are many, many functions in a marriage: coach, confidant, cheerleader, chore-handler,
locater-of-strange-night-noises, etc. But the most crucial function to remember is a teammate.

Intimacy – both emotional and physical – is the fuel of a marriage.

In most cases, it's important to think that, no matter what the outcome was, your spouse probably intended the best.

The adorable little behaviors you adore about your partner, in the beginning, will, after a few years together, be the cause of lunacy.

When you marry your spouse, you marry their family and all that comes with it. Act appropriately.
It's not enough to take care of your partner. You also have to care for yourself.
You can — and will — say garbage about your relationship with others. But when others speak garbage about them, it will fill you with wrath.
If you're not attempting to better yourself, you're not working to improve your marriage.
At some time, you'll chat to your single buddies and think Man, that's the life. Equally as frequently, you'll chat to your single pals and think They don't realize what they're missing.
The ugly reality of life after marriage is primarily about the brutal truth of life after kids.

Chances are, a guy will not alter too much after marriage and post kids. A lady, though, will undoubtedly do a lot of altering. Once babies are born, most women become "mommy first, wife second". Most spouses, on the other hand, just seem to keep rolling along as their old selves, albeit their old selves with kids.

Many men would remark that their marriage was very well finished after the first kid was born. Well, it is true. The partnership, as you knew it before kids, is finished. Gone. When a guy feels ignored – which is typically the end consequence – he either closes up and hides in the basement or the booze cupboard, or seeks someone who will make him feel respected and important again (i.e., cheating). That is the ugly fact of life after marriage if a guy feels ignored.

The harsh fact from a woman's viewpoint, after marriage and kids, is that women wind up doing the lion's share of the labor. They perform most of the parenting, most of the planning and scheduling of family life, most of the housekeeping, most of the shopping, most of the cooking, and most of the chauffeuring. They commonly get divorced. The mom feels insulted, underappreciated, let down, and bitter. That is the unpleasant fact of life after marriage if a working mom is left to perform most of the labor at home.

None of this needs to be the case. Marriages that endure, and that are pleasant, have a "Marriage 1 and a Marriage 2" type of dynamic.

If you strive to make your post-kid marriage feel like a pre-kid marriage, you will probably fail. The trick is to create a new marriage, which is also full of love, appreciation, respect, and fun, within the post-kid reality which includes a very needy young human being, a lot of tedium, patience galore, and the non-stop hard work of living within a family system without a lot of help from outside (for most people).

There is nothing harsh about having a tiny family of your own. It is wonderful. But it requires a lot of hard work, continual communication, sharing of your emotions, and being intuitive about what makes your spouse happy and what makes your spouse sad.

If you are thinking about having kids, you and your husband need to think long and hard about what your duties will be in terms of the job of parenting. Talk details, not just generalities (such as "50%/50%"). Who will do what? The chores don't need to be equal; simply clear and divvied up in a manner that eliminates resentment. Do what you say you are going to do and be appreciative of each other for all your hard work (whether your spouse does the task "your way" your not).

Chapter 2

How to make sure your marriage withstands changes

Relationships naturally evolve as they grow and develop. Dealing with changes begins with knowing your spouse and discovering methods to handle differences.

Navigating relationships with your spouse is undoubtedly one of the toughest and most intricate elements of the human experience.

Although it's normal for change to happen in a marriage, sometimes it may be difficult for one or both parties to understand why and what to do about it.

The subsequent aggravation and fighting may make you feel that your relationship troubles are impossible to solve. The good news is, that if you spend some time understanding the core reasons for relationship change, you can find strategies to work through it together.

Why changes happen

Marriages go through numerous phases as they mature. While this is occurring, you and your spouse may also endure stressful life events, such as health challenges, financial troubles, and disagreements with friends or family members.

Sometimes life events are exciting - like relocating to a new town or receiving a new job. But even good circumstances may produce relational issues.

According to studies in 2017, stresses may adversely affect relationship satisfaction, whether the stress originates from inside the partnership or from outside.

What are changes you could encounter in a relationship?
Some changes that occur in partnerships are more profound than others. For example, substantial changes may include:

One of you no longer wants to have children.
Your lover wants to live someplace you don't.
Your significant other discovers they aren't monogamous, identifies as another gender, or no longer has the same sexual preferences you have.
Your companion has a new physical or mental health issue.
However, sometimes apparently modest adjustments might trigger a shift in relationships. These include:

Your companion joins the gym or adopts a new activity.
One of you makes a new acquaintance.
You or your partner's work schedule changes.

Annoying behaviors begin to appear for the first time.

Many of these changes simply occur from the normal phases a relationship goes through as it matures. So, it would assist to understand what these phases are, and how you could feel as you traverse them.

How connections develop

In general, there are several frequently regarded phases a marriage may go through while it's evolving.

1. The infatuation or "honeymoon" period

Intoxicating and all-encompassing, this is the early period of a marriage when you can't seem to get enough of one other.

Although the sensation is heavenly, this period is also when both individuals are on their best behavior — therefore it may be tough to identify any undesirable tendencies in the other. It's likely where the expression "blinded by love" arose.

2. The power struggle or disillusionment stage
This period is hallmarked by natural changes that might be challenging to handle.

What previously seemed charming in your spouse might become bothersome. Differences in values and life objectives become obvious, and the love blindness experienced in the infatuation stage is now replaced with a 20/20 vision.

Here's where most couples may begin to wonder about everything about the relationship and even question if it should continue.

3. The commitment stage
Once the bumpy road commonly traversed in the previous stage has receded, your

partnership may enter a time of understanding and mutual respect.

You both know you can't change the other and also learn to embrace your differences. Of course, this stage isn't immune to obstacles brought on by life circumstances, but you and your spouse are now more ready to face them as they emerge.

4. The co-creation stage
As time goes on and your partnership has withstood a few storms, a spirit of teamwork takes hold. As a determined team, you and your spouse understand each other and begin to take on the world together.

This stage isn't without its problems. However, a 2014 research exploring marital lifespan reveals couples are less likely to split up the longer they've been together.

Is change in a relationship bad?

It's not always a terrible thing when a relationship changes — depending on how you or your partner manage it.

Sometimes changes are excellent, like acquiring a new job or adopting healthy lifestyle choices like joining a gym.

Despite being a beneficial change, you might have a hard time adjusting to any form of change.

For instance, your partner's promotion at work may be a welcomed change, but it also comes with hard work hours. If you or your spouse are having a hard time with this new schedule, it might create pressure in the relationship.

Some changes, though, aren't necessarily positive.

For example, assume your spouse was affectionate and attentive at the beginning of the relationship but, with time, turns abusive. This unfavorable alteration might impact the relationship at its core.

Whether your spouse has changed in a manner that causes you mental or bodily pain in any way, consider reevaluating your relationship to see if it's no longer a safe condition for you.

Dealing with change

If anything is suddenly new in your relationship — large or little — here are a few guidelines to help you handle it effectively.

Investigate plausible explanations for the change

Certain changes in you or your spouse might be a clue that they're developing a medical or mental health problem like depression. If you feel this is the case, try approaching them with empathy and asking if there's anything you can do to assist.

In other circumstances, your partner's behavioral changes may not represent a shift at all. Instead, it may be something they've always done, but now — for whatever reason — it's beginning to bother you.

In this instance, consider doing some soul-searching into whether this is something you can tolerate. If it isn't, you might attempt to express this with your spouse to come up with a solution or compromise that works for both of you.

Zero in on the root issue

One technique to cope with a relationship that's changed is to ask yourself: What is it specifically about this difference that worries me? Once you establish what it is, you can then articulate your concerns more effectively.

For example, instead of stating, "I detest this new buddy you have," you may explain to your partner: "I'm delighted you found someone you enjoy hanging out with, but I feel like we aren't spending as much time together as I'd like."

Communicate to comprehend
When things don't quite seem right in a relationship, communication is the key to understanding the other partner's viewpoint.

For large changes like a spouse that suddenly doesn't want to have children anymore, this might require delving into various reasons why.

For instance, maybe they genuinely do want children, but they're concerned they'll be unable to maintain them financially. Once you understand the causes behind this transformation, you may work together to lessen their anxieties.

Don't concentrate on your partner's flaws
Many couples report that the spouse changes after marriage or the female body changes after marriage.

As we know that the only constant in life is 'change', therefore never be swayed away by external looks. The human body is perishable and vulnerable to change over time. Accept it gently and compassionately!

Count your blessings
Instead of brooding on things that change when you are married, why not appreciate the benefits that we have been married?

Always attempt to focus on the good features of your mate. Of course, it isn't simple but is doable if you practice optimism continuously.

Stop comparing before and after marriage Consider each era of your life as a separate chapter. To move on in life and gain new experiences, you have to move on to the next chapter, by letting go of the previous chapter in your life.

With a new chapter, comes new experiences. To appreciate them to the utmost, you have to stop comparing your past and the present. They both can never be the same. Relationships are like living things – they develop and change with the seasons of life.

Embracing change and learning to adjust when expectations aren't fulfilled helps guarantee your relationships continue to grow the way it was intended to.

Chapter 3

How to tackle typical marital troubles

All the movies we have watched growing up—from Snow White to Titanic—have given our globe a window into what genuine love should look like. Women are yearning for their Prince Charming since our environment tends to exalt marriage.

As a consequence, marriage appears like a decent decision for most individuals. After all, why shouldn't it? Who wouldn't want to ride off into the sunset together and live happily ever after?

But the movies make it appear simple. And as any married person will tell you, marriage in real life is oftentimes anything but simple. In fact, for many couples, it may be downright terrible if they don't know how to work through their difficulties.

And think about it—no one teaches us how to have a happy, healthy marriage. If our parents didn't model it for us, then we have no idea how to do it ourselves.

Because of this, practically all marriages experience troubles. Some couples are better at dealing with the ups and downs over the years than others, but they all have them.

Most married couples have comparable concerns. So, let's take a look at some of the most common problems most marriages face.

1. Division of Labor
Research shows that even when both spouses work outside the home, the woman is usually the one who does more of the housework and chores.

This produces extra stress for her. But what's even more burdensome than these regular responsibilities is termed "psychological responsibility." In other words, women are expected to remember things like "Johnny has a doctor's appointment on Tuesday," or "We have to attend Jane's soccer game on Saturday at 2:00."

While it's not usually the woman who performs more of the job, a lack of balance with the division of labor may generate a lot of troubles.

Average Couples See Chores as a Cornerstone, Happy Couples See Them as the Gem Stone

2. Finances

Some folks are spenders. Others are savers. So, if you have a spender and a saver together in a marriage, you can see how it might create an issue.

Maybe producing and investing money is vital to one individual, while the other couldn't care less about it. Fighting about money and how it is spent is one of the most typical difficulties in marriages.

3. Children and Parenting Differences
Let's face it—children can be stressed! The crying/sleepless newborns, temper tantrums, and rebellious adolescents are not a lot of fun sometimes, regardless of how much you love your kids! And it may bring a lot of stress to a marriage. Even contrasting parenting techniques like how to reprimand a kid may create a split in a married relationship.

4. Personality Differences
If one person is an introvert and the other is an extrovert, then there may be ongoing conflict over how frequently to socialize.

The extrovert could feel neglected because the introvert never wants to go to a party with them. But the introvert could feel rejected since the extrovert constantly wants to associate with others other than their spouse. And this is only one facet of personality differences that might create issues in relationships.

5. Fighting and Communication Style Differences

Maybe one spouse grew up in a home where they shouted and screamed at each other when they were furious, while the other spouse grew up in a family that turned their emotions inside and would give people quiet treatment. Maintaining distinct fighting or communication styles when it comes to disputes may be a significant impediment to having a happy and healthy marriage.

6. Different Love Languages

There are five distinct ways individuals offer and receive love (acts of service, touch, time, giving of gifts, words of encouragement) (acts of service, touch, time, giving of gifts, and words of affirmation). If you both speak highly different love languages, you could not feel loved by your spouse, which may lead to marital troubles.

For example, if you want to be given presents to feel loved but instead your spouse would rather conduct acts of service for you—like repairing your vehicle or soothing your feet—then you may not comprehend that they truly do love you.

7. Sex

Everyone has varied sexual needs—both in frequency and kind. Some individuals adore having sex as frequently as they can, while others could spend the rest of their lives without it. And some require a lot of kinky things to be pleased. Regardless matter what you desire, most couples have an issue with their sexual compatibility.

8. Jealousy and Infidelity

Many individuals are inherently insecure and sadly, many people are also inclined to cheat on their spouses. So, whether or not someone cheats, there may be envy that occurs inside the relationship.

Infidelity isn't simply confined to physical infidelity though. Emotional infidelity is running rampant these days because of technology, such as phones and dating apps. They make it so simple to disguise what someone is doing and whom they are talking to.

9. Boredom
Relationships are usually thrilling when they are fresh. Everyone feels like they are walking on cloud 9 because they are so in love. But then as time goes on, the newness and infatuation fade off. As that occurs, many couples go into a slump. Their relationship stagnates and begins to grow uninteresting. It takes work to attempt to keep the love alive and to keep doing interesting things together.

10. Power Inequity

Power may come in many forms—from financial authority to parental power. If one spouse produces more money than the other (or maybe one is a stay-at-home parent), that creates an imbalance when it comes to who brings in the money. And this imbalance is a common marriage problem.

Who has more decision-making power? Many times, it's not equal. So, it presents difficulties because one of the spouses might grow to feel weak over time.

11. Abuse

Abuse can occur in numerous ways. Physical abuse is what most people think of when they hear the term abuse. But mental and emotional abuse is also highly destructive to persons and the partnership as a whole: The Invisible Violence in Relationships That Destroys People

When one or both individuals are not respecting one another by putting their hands on them or using nasty language when they talk, it may rip up a marriage in no time.

12. Values and Beliefs
As the proverb goes, "a bird and a fish may love one other, but where will they live?" In other words, when two individuals have extremely different ways of looking at the world, it makes it difficult to comprehend one another. And this may lead to troubles in marriage.

For example, if a Catholic is married to a Muslim, they generally don't share a lot of ideas and worldviews. If they both have different political views, it may generate huge conflict in a marriage as well.

13. Trying to Change Each Other
No one is perfect. There will always be something about everyone in the world that

will bother you. But when people don't comprehend this, then they strive to alter each other.

They think, "I can't tolerate that Bob doesn't want to go to the gym and work out with me, but after we get married, I'll alter his mind." No. That NEVER works! You cannot alter people.

So, you should simply learn to accept each other the way you are. Otherwise, you would be making each other unhappy with all of the naggings that go into attempting to change a person—and anyway, it's simply not feasible.

14. Keeping Score

If someone feels like they are doing significantly more for the other person than they are for them, then it's natural to keep track.

You think, “I work, and then I come home and cook and clean and take care of the kids. But all the time, Ben is just sitting on the sofa, sipping his beer, and not even realizing how stressed up I am!” Then in your mind, you believe you have piled up a lot more on the scoreboard than he has. As a consequence, anger builds up over time and it may damage a marriage.

15. Unrealistic Expectations
We all have a concept of how we want other people to behave.
For example, maybe you believe that when someone is married, they should have sex every day. But let’s face it—most couples are fatigued from work, kids, housework, etc. So, it doesn’t happen.

Maybe you believe your wife should prepare gourmet meals all the time just like your parents did. Well, maybe she hates to cook! Putting unreasonable expectations on your partner will merely make you both unhappy and resentful.

16. Immaturity
Great partnerships are intended to evolve. If you still connect the same way you did when you first married, then it's past time for the marriage to grow up. Love one another "out loud." Invest in the marriage as if your life depended on it — because it does.

17. Moving
It's a fact. Most individuals change occupations multiple times. That typically means migrating across the state or the globe. Moving is a major hardship. Regardless of whether it's due to your work or your spouse's, choose to be 100% supportive and flat-out refuse to whinge. Do all it takes to become immersed in the new community fast. Find a church. Get engaged. Live forward.

18. Sickness

We forget how much we rely on one another until someone breaks down physically. If you're the one still standing, do all in your ability to be a servant to your spouse. Sure it's challenging to complete everything, but your try with an evident eager attitude is going to make all the difference.

19. Empty Nest:\sWe invest a lot in the kids. If we're not cautious, our connection with our spouse goes ignored. Guard against that day by investing in your marriage today. Rather than lament the children once they go, consider enjoying the freedom you now have to devote more time and interest to your marriage. Again, it's all about being deliberate.

20. Daily Stress

Daily pressures don't need to equal marital issues, but they might worsen problems that already exist. When one spouse has had a stressful day, they may be more likely to be impatient when they come home, may manage disputes less skillfully, and may have the less emotional energy to give to nourishing their relationship. When both spouses have had a terrible day, this of course is simply aggravated.

As with financial stress, general everyday stress may limit tolerance and optimism, leaving couples with less to contribute to one another emotionally.

All relationships and marriages go through phases when they experience issues. The key to a good and flourishing relationship is your capacity to overcome these obstacles. The instant you turn your back on your relationship when you confront marital troubles, it will swiftly slip into despair. Solving marital difficulties can not only make your relationship better but also more robust.

Chapter 4

Strategies for Solving Marital Problems

All marriages have issues, but not every couple can work through them. These are the best techniques to fix your marital difficulties, no matter what it is that is producing the challenges.

1. COMMUNICATE, COMMUNICATE, COMMUNICATE
Communication is the cornerstone of a lasting relationship. All healthy and happy couples maintain their communication channels open.

If you are attempting to fix your marital troubles, you should not cease interacting with your spouse. Openly address the challenges you are experiencing so that you may come up with a resolution together. If you simply brush it under a rug, it will only blossom into something more severe in the long term.

techniques to assist fix your marital troubles

2. RECOGNIZE WHEN YOU'RE IN A GRIDLOCK

One of the most typical difficulties in fixing marriage problems is when you and your spouse don't see eye to eye when it comes to your marital challenges. One spouse is ready to address the topic while the other doesn't see it as a significant concern.

When you've hit a stalemate, it's vital to take a pause. Forcing your viewpoint on things won't alter the circumstance. By taking a break, you offer time for each of you to put things in perspective.

3. EXPRESS YOURSELF CONSTRUCTIVELY

When you are in an argument with your spouse, it is tempting to let your emotions take control. You might wind yourself saying nasty words that just compound the situation instead of addressing them. Try to avoid this path whenever feasible.

When addressing your marital troubles, concentrate on being helpful. It is also vital to keep on-topic and not to bring up earlier concerns.

4. BREAK THE CURSE OF FAMILIARITY

Married couples who have been together for a long period have this erroneous impression that they know each other thoroughly. However, this may frequently be the source of the issue in a relationship.

Never stop asking questions or seeking to get to know your companion. This can help you understand their needs better and assist prevent conflict, or grasp their viewpoint when it comes to addressing difficulties inside your marriage.

There will be less tension in your relationship if you know where your spouse is coming from.

5. MAKE DECISIONS TOGETHER

When you are tackling marital difficulties, you need to approach them jointly and decide on the best solution as a pair. One spouse cannot be dictatorial and make choices for the two of you. In reality, this is something that creates marital troubles in the first place.

By making choices jointly, you may both be at peace knowing that you've considered your partner's thoughts and worries. Avoid the impulse to insist on what you want or do things your way. Keep an open mind and encourage your partner to speak their viewpoint.

If things start to become hot between you in an argument, think of methods to de-escalate the dispute and try to keep things light.

6. ACKNOWLEDGE YOUR SPOUSE'S FEELINGS

Have you ever encountered speaking up about your emotions and then having those sentiments shut down or dismissed? It's not a nice sensation. It makes you feel unappreciated and overlooked.

You don't want your partner to feel this way. If you are seeking to overcome problems inside your marriage, you need to support one another. Allow your spouse to speak out and make their emotions known. Even if you don't agree with them, don't discount their sentiments. Instead, attempt to put yourself in their place and understand why they feel that way. Look at what you can do to address such emotions. That is what couples in healthy marriages do.

7. UNDERSTAND THAT IT'S NOT A COMPETITION

It is not unusual for couples to feel the need to 'win' a disagreement. It feeds their ego and helps them feel good about themselves when they show their partner incorrect on some topics.

You should not fix your marriage difficulties with this type of mindset. Often, if you win an argument, your relationship loses. This should not be about who wins or loses; concentrate on addressing flaws in your marriage so you may both be happy and healthy.

8. KEEP A POSITIVE ATTITUDE

This may seem like an easy idea but most couples who are arguing find it difficult to remain upbeat. Successful couples are the ones who can retain a positive viewpoint throughout their relationship even while coping with marital challenges.

The fact that you and your spouse are taking measures to address your concerns is a positive indicator. This should urge you to keep hopeful about the future of your partnership. Hold on to that optimism and discover methods to preserve your relationship, particularly if you both agree that it's worth keeping.

9. GIVE YOUR PARTNER SPACE

Most partners are so determined to settle conflicts inside their marriage that they end up suffocating their other half. However, employing this method while you are coping with marital troubles can only make matters worse.

Give your partner the room to ponder and reflect. It will also provide you the chance to look at things from their viewpoint. When you give each other space, you don't behave primarily on feelings but rather on logic and thinking.

10. GET COUNSELING.

Counseling is an excellent technique to address marital difficulties. It will take a few sessions only, and is a terrific approach to discuss difficulties within your relationship on a neutral ground. You may also acquire the help of an expert so you can find out the reason for the issue.

The key to success with therapy is to follow through with the strategy. Any consultation you've done with a therapist will be of little help if you have no responsibility and don't follow through with it. Both couples must accept responsibility for addressing their marital difficulties.

If you think therapy is costly, it's surely cheaper than divorce! Plus, if you are serious about fixing marital difficulties, this is one of the finest methods to go about it.

Bottom Line

No one has a flawless marriage—not even the ones who are the happiest! Being happy while being married involves work, but it doesn't imply that effort has to be hard.

If you both attempt to offer 100% to work through the inevitable marital challenges that you confront, then the marriage may function well. It takes a lot of devotion and love, but it can be done.

www.ingramcontent.com/pod-product-compliance
Lightning Source LLC
LaVergne TN
LVHW020525160826
845677LV00015B/3907

* 9 7 9 8 3 5 2 0 0 6 7 6 4 *